ALLEN PHOTOGRAPHIC GUIDES

RIDING
A DRESSAGE TEST

CONTENTS

THE JUDGE'S VIEWPOINT

WHAT THE DRESSAGE JUDGE WANTS TO SEE

1. Rhythm
2. Suppleness
3. Acceptance of the bridle
4. Impulsion
5. Straightness
6. Collection
7. Rider position

A fuller explanation of these scales of training is covered in the J. A. Allen photo guide *Preparing for a Dressage Test*, which complements this book.

This novice horse shows good balance and activity in competition.

Note *Please see page 23 for a diagram of a dressage arena.*

PRELIMINARY

THE ENTRY

First impressions do matter and, with dressage tests, that impression will be made as the horse and rider enter the arena and proceed up the centre line.

The Competitor enters the test arena at **A**. In Preliminary and Novice tests this is at working trot, and in many instances no halt or salute is required. This gives the horse the chance to make a good entry, moving forward and straight. In Elementary tests the entry is usually ridden in collected trot and a halt and salute is required. When riding the entry and to encourage better straightness, the rider asks the horse to go actively forwards within the working or collected trot.

The judge expects to see that the horse is straight, forwards and in good rhythm. These photographs show some errors to avoid: veering

off the centre line (a); crooked on the centre line (b); off the centre line altogether (c).

CORNERS AND TURNS

Every corner, well ridden, offers the rider opportunities to improve the horse's engagement and balance. From the judge's perspective, how a horse moves through corners shows the correctness of the horse's training and the skills of the rider. Turns are similar to corners in as much as they are a portion of a circle.

Turns and corners present difficulties if the riding and training are incorrect. For example, if the rider pulls on the inside rein to make a turn it will unbalance the horse, and if the turn is before a straight line (such as the centre line) then the errors become clear to the judge. The horse will fall onto his shoulder, wiggle a little to regain balance, then, perhaps, move straight but, shortly afterwards, he will meet another turn and, if the rider pulls on the inside rein again, there will be another loss of balance and another wiggle! These errors make it easy to lose marks and yet

> **DAVID'S TIP**
>
> In Preliminary and Novice tests the rider can choose whether to go in rising or sitting trot and can fluctuate between both throughout a test. In Elementary tests no rising trot is allowed.

it is something that is easily corrected. If the horse is ridden in balance before, and during, the turns he will be able to show: better straightness and better impulsion, and he has a good chance of keeping self-carriage throughout corners and turns.

Preparing to ride through a corner

The quarter markers (**F, H, M, K**) are positioned 6 m before the end of each long side of the arena. These quarter markers act like indicator lights to the rider. They say: 'prepare the horse so he can move around the corner in good rhythm, balance and straightness'. The rider primes the horse's balance through a half-halt and this will be by applying the inside-leg-to-outside-rein aids.

Body bend

When moving through a corner, the horse's body should follow the curve of the corner so that he remains on two tracks. In photo (a) the horse is on three tracks. The muscles on the inside of his body contract and those on the outside stretch. This enables his body to follow the line of the corner. To do this requires suppleness and straightness. The horse should be equally supple and straight on both sides of his body and the judge will be looking for this throughout the test.

Avoid pulling on the inside rein

This puts the horse out of balance and allows him to drift through his outside shoulder (b). When the inside rein is pulled strongly it can make the horse go so crooked that he moves on three tracks (c). The judge would mark this strictly since the horse *must always move straight*, i.e. the back feet follow in the tracks of the front feet, unless lateral work is required, e.g. three-track shoulder-in (*see* pages 19–20).

The outside rein

The horse must accept the outside rein contact. It is critical that the rider asks for the correct amount of outside rein in the right circumstances otherwise the horse will become unbalanced or lose straightness or inside bend.

The inside rein can never be applied well without outside rein contact; inside rein without outside rein negates the effect of inside bend. If the outside rein is not used there will be too much neck bend to the inside to support the horse and the energy is lost through the outside shoulder. Consequently the horse becomes crooked (*see below*).

The outside rein must provide a consistent elastic contact between the rider's hand and the horse's mouth which allows inside bend (*see below*). If, on the other hand, the outside rein is held too tightly, it prevents inside flexion and body bend and can result in flexion to the outside. Outside flexion is incorrect in a test

unless an exercise specifically requires it, e.g. counter canter or trot loops or unless the horse's poll is suppled in that direction momentarily.

Balanced and in rhythm through the corner

The judge expects to see the horse approach, go into, through and exit the corner in the same rhythm and balance.

Sometimes, the rider may need to refresh the horse's balance by a half-halt. A well-ridden corner will increase the horse's engagement and balance and prepare him for the next movement.

DAVID'S TIP

Each test sheet is sectioned off and numbered, the following example is from a Preliminary test.

4.   E   Circle left 20 m diameter
     EK   Working trot 10

This means the competitor must ride a 20m circle at the **E** marker of the arena and continue in working trot until **K**. The judge awards marks to a maximum of 10 for this section. Straight lines, turns, corners, circles and other figure riding, transitions and the three gaits of walk, trot and canter are incorporated into dressage tests. Their difficulty depends on the standard of the test being ridden, for example, at Preliminary level, large circles, 5m loops and 10m half-circles are required in working trot whereas at Elementary level the competitor is required to show collected, working and medium trot and sometimes shoulder-in.

TROT LOOPS AND SERPENTINES

Trot Loops
(E.g. in working trot, between K and H, one loop 5 m in from the track.)

The competitor starts the loop at **K** showing good inside bend. The loop reaches its maximum (i.e. 5 m) distance from the track when passing **E**. Just before **E** the rider straightens the inside bend and asks the horse for outside bend until **H**. At **H** inside bend is resumed.

The judge expects to see 1. correct degrees of inside and outside bend; 2. accuracy of the movement (i.e. the first part of the loop is the same as the second part); 3. the rhythm of the working trot remains consistent; 4. the balance remains consistent.

This horse shows the correct bend for the second half of a trot loop on the left rein.

Trot serpentines
(E.g. at A serpentine three loops, each loop to go to the long side of the arena finishing at C.)

The competitor starts the movement at **A** on the left rein and rides so that the horse meets the track just after **F** moving on the track for a few strides before turning in a round loop across the arena halfway between **K** and **E**. On crossing the centre line the bend is changed from left to right inside bend and, if in rising trot, the horse's trot diagonal is changed from left to right. At **E** the horse touches the track for a few strides before turning across the school halfway between **B** and **M**. The rider changes the inside bend, this time from right to left and the horse's trot diagonal if in rising trot. The last loop of the serpentine is completed by the horse moving for a few strides on the track just before M and the exercise is completed at **C**.

The judge expects to see, as with trot loops, that correct bend is shown on each change of direction, that the trot is in good rhythm and the serpentine is accurate, and that the horse's balance is maintained throughout the changes of direction of each of the loops.

CANTER TO TROT TRANSITIONS

These are carried out in various places within the arena in the lower level tests and are more difficult when asked for on the diagonal across the arena. *(E.g. MXK change the rein [in working canter], between X and K working trot.)*

The competitor ideally asks for the transition just after **X**, rebalancing the trot before **K** and then rebalancing the horse again in the corner.

The judge expects to see that the horse makes the turn at the top of the diagonal (in this instance at M) smoothly and that the canter rhythm remains intact, the transition to trot is made in balance, i.e. without the horse rushing off, or falling on his forehand, or coming to trot before X. Once in the trot, the quality of the trot must be maintained.

FREE WALK ON A LONG REIN

(E.g. MXK change rein at free walk on a long rein.)

This horse shows an excellent free walk on a long rein with good overtracking, and good stretching and lowering which allows freedom of the head, neck and back.

The competitor asks the horse to turn into the diagonal of the arena at **M** and then asks him to march forwards in front of the seat. At the same time the rider allows the reins to slip through the fingers. If the horse is working 'through' his back correctly and moving forwards actively he should seek the bit by stretching his head and neck down and forwards towards the ground with his nose slightly in front of the vertical. Shortly before **K** the rider takes up the reins and asks the horse to accept the contact and make the transition from the free walk to the medium walk.

The judge expects to see that the transitions to and from the free walk are good and smooth (i.e. without any signs of jogging or loss of the four-beat walk rhythm, and that the horse's back and neck are rounded, which allows maximum opportunity for relaxation and a chance to show a clear overtracking of the footfalls without losing the four-time walk rhythm.

DAVID'S TIPS

In front of the seat The horse's response to the aids must never be dull nor should he lean against the leg or hand and use the aids as a prop; hence the term 'in front of' when referring to the horse's response to the rider's seat or leg aids.

Through The horse is said to be 'through' when the energy created by the hind legs flows uninterruptedly forwards through his body, over a supple back and neck, without resistance, or hesitation, and draws forward into an elastic contact.

The coefficient Double marks (a coefficient) are awarded for some parts of the tests. At Preliminary, Novice and Elementary levels they apply to *free walk on a long rein* and at Elementary also to the *extended walk*, where the walk strides cover as much ground as possible. The activity should be without haste. One of the reasons for giving a coefficient is that in every test there are less movements ridden in the walk than the trot and canter. By giving a coefficient to the walk the weighting of the marks is better balanced and the test more fair.

In the more advanced tests *collected walk* is required when, often, the judge will see the walk rhythm disrupted. When this happens a low mark must be awarded. The coefficient is then given to the extended walk where the horse can be rewarded for his true movement.

MEDIUM WALK

The judge expects the horse's natural walk to be expressed with a touch more energy, and that he overtracks and maintains the integrity of the walk rhythm. The horse should be soft on the contact.

Medium walk half-circles with a change of rein *(E.g. at A medium walk, BX half-circle left 10m diameter, XE half-circle right 10m diameter.)*

The competitor starts the first half-circle coming off the track at **B**. The horse follows the line of the 10 m half-circle, inside bend is shown to the left. The horse is made straight on the centre line for a stride before and after **X** and then follows the line of the right 10m half-circle.

This horse shows good bend in the first half-circle (*see below*) and in the change of direction (*see right*).

The judge expects to see changes of inside bend from the first half-circle to the second one, and that the bend is equal on both reins, that the horse keeps a good rhythm to the medium walk, maintains a soft, accepting contact with the bit, remains on two tracks throughout the movement and that the movement is ridden accurately.

CIRCLES IN TROT AND CANTER

In Preliminary tests the circles in trot and canter are kept large and at the maximum width the arena permits. (Arena sizes are 20 x 40 m for most of the lower level competitions and some Elementary and Medium tests, and 20 x 60 m for all other tests.) *(E.g. At **C** circle left 20 m diameter.)*

The competitor takes the horse into the corner before **C**, starting the circle at **C**. The rider gets a correct shape to the circle by riding towards four points on the circle and by riding an arc between each of these four points. In this example, the first point is at **C**, the second halfway between the first corner and **E**, the third at **X** and the fourth halfway between **B** and the corner before **C**. The circle is finished at **C**. The intelligent rider checks the horse goes well into the corner after **C**, which shows the difference between the circle and the corner.

The judge expects to see that the circle shape is accurate and the rhythm of the gait remains true and full of impulsion and that the horse accepts the contact and moves on two tracks.

DAVID'S TIP

Riding the circle with four points gives a line to the circle and helps you aim for a round, correct shape. Providing you sit correctly, i.e. you look to the line of the circle so that your body weight stays in balance with the horse and you do not interfere with the horse's straightness by pulling on the inside rein or holding the outside contact too tightly, the circle shape should be correct. Make sure you differentiate between the line of a circle and the turn through a corner. Do not confuse the two.

THE EXIT

Last impressions count as much as first impressions!
*(E.g. at **A** down centre line, **G** halt, immobility, salute,
leave the arena at walk on a long rein.)*

The competitor rides the horse down the centre
line in the gait required in the test (at Preliminary
and Novice levels this is mostly working trot). The
horse is ridden forwards into a halt and stands still
for a few seconds in immobility. The rider takes the
reins and whip (if being carried) into one hand and
salutes the judge. It is incorrect for the whip to be
in the free (saluting) hand (*see right*). Women
salute by raising a hand then lowering it by the
hip and, at the same time, nodding the head. For
men the salute is similar but the hat is removed
and held in the free hand (*see right, below*).

After saluting, the rider walks the horse forwards
on a long rein and heads back towards **A** (*see
below*). It is quite permissible to pat the horse, but
remember that the test is not completed until the
exit at **A** and so the competitor must be careful
not to speak or allow any outside influences to
interfere, which could result in lost marks.

The judge expects to see that the horse moves
forwards to a square and straight halt, remains on
the aids in the halt and immobility (i.e. he does not
fidget or move from his position) and that the rider
salutes according to the etiquette of dressage. The
horse leaves the arena calmly.

NOVICE

TROT LENGTHENING

(E.g. HXF change the rein [in working trot] and progressively show some lengthened strides. At F working trot.)

The competitor balances the horse in the corner before **H** checking he is active and engaged before the turn at **H**. He refreshes the engagement by asking for a little more roundness and activity in the trot for the first three strides across the diagonal and then applies the leg aids and asks for some lengthened trot strides (*see right*), keeping the seat supple in order to go with the increased movement through the horse's back. As the horse starts to lengthen, the rider's hands follow the contact with an elastic feel but should not drop the contact because this tends to allow the horse to fall on his forehand. To prepare the horse for the transition to working trot the rider sits deeper and closes the legs and hands approximately three strides before **F** and then refreshes this engagement into a good working trot at **F**.

The judge expects to see that the horse steps forward more into equal lengthened strides. (The movement is equal if the angle of the forearm to the ground matches the angle of the hind leg cannon bone to the ground.) In Novice tests the judge would prefer to see a handful of well-balanced lengthened strides rather than the whole diagonal of huge unbalanced ones.

The competitor has already progressively introduced the horse to the half-halts in training through transitions and half-transitions. The rider prepares the horse for a transition to walk by sitting deeper, taking the hips forwards and keeping the seat supple and not stiffening against the horse. At the moment the rider feels the energy come through the horse's back to his withers the hands are closed for a fraction of a second. If a rider is not experienced enough to feel this movement of energy, a split-second delay should be allowed before the hands are closed. The feeling in the hand should remain soft and elastic, the horse accepting the few seconds of increased contact gracefully. The walk moves forwards for 2–4 steps, then the rider applies the aids for trot (i.e. sits tall, closes the lower leg and thinks forward with the hands without dropping the steady elastic contact).

TROT TO WALK TO TROT TRANSITIONS

(E.g. BF working trot. Between F and A transition to walk [2–4 steps] and immediately proceed at working trot.)

This movement shows the start of half-halts.

DAVID'S TIP

This movement highlights the importance of the progressive training to teaching the horse the half-halt and is very much an integral part of test riding and dressage training.

How quickly the rider needs to apply the upward transition aids depends on the responsiveness of each individual horse and the timing of these aids should have been fine-tuned prior to the competition.

The judge expects to see that the horse moves forwards through a soft back into a forward downward transition, remaining in balance, and responds promptly to the aids for the transition upwards to trot.

This Preliminary level horse shows good self-carriage at working trot.

TROT 10 m HALF-CIRCLES TO CENTRE LINE RETURNING TO THE TRACK AT THE HALF-MARKER

(E.g. MBF working trot. At F half-circle right 10 m diameter, returning to the track at B.)

The competitor rides a half-circle from **F** keeping the inside bend and on touching **D** at the centre line rides straight back on a diagonal line to the **B** marker, where he then changes flexion.

The judge expects to see that the working-trot rhythm remains regular throughout the turns, that the bend and change of bend are correct and that the horse is on two tracks when on the diagonal line.

IN WORKING CANTER, GIVE AND RETAKE THE REINS

(E.g. in working canter right, 20 m circle at A, give and retake the reins.)

This photo shows good giving of the reins, however the horse is on the forehand.

In some tests, this exercise will be asked for across the diagonal. *(E.g. in working canter right, MXK, change the rein, give and retake the reins over X. At K working trot.)*

The competitor sits quietly to the canter with a supple seat not disturbing the rhythm through the turn at **M**. The reins are given a few strides over **X** by the rider pushing the hands forwards up the horse's crest, and then allowing the horse to canter with the reins held like this for at least three to four canter strides. Then the reins are retaken into the normal riding position and the contact resumed. A half-halt a few strides before **K** warns the horse of a pending change in gait so that the trot transition can be made at **K**.

This horse is above the bit with no self-carriage. We see him gaining speed and rushing off.

The judge expects to see that the horse is in self-carriage and keeps the same outline and rhythm in the canter (i.e. does not come above the bit or rush off as the above photo shows). Keeping good balance is reflected in the horse's capacity to make a forward, smooth transition to trot at **K**. He must not fall on his forehand nor respond to the downward transition too late, or too soon before **K**. The movement should be accurate and appear smooth, free flowing and tidy.

CANTER 15 M HALF-CIRCLE

(E.g. just before M half-circle left [in working canter left] 15 m diameter returning to the track between B and F. At F working trot.)

The competitor starts preparing for the 15 m half-circle so that its maximum size is reached 5 m in from the track opposite **H**, and then returns straight back to the track after **B** so that 2–4 counter-canter strides can be shown before the trot transition at **F**.

The judge expects to see that the movement is accurate, the rhythm good and that the horse

can show the beginnings of counter canter without loss of balance and bend to the outside.

The Elementary horse below shows the degree of counter-canter bend needed for the exercise. He is ridden in a double bridle. From Elementary level upwards, competitors can use either a snaffle or a double bridle but, at Preliminary and Novice levels, a snaffle must be used. At Advanced level the double bridle is compulsory.

DAVID'S TIP

The 15 m half-circle needs to be positioned so that it nearly touches the track near to **C**. Be careful not to return to the track too close to **B** because it gives too sharp an angle for the return to the track, but do allow enough room for the trot transition after a few counter-canter strides. **Note** Only a little bend is needed for counter canter and the bend is to the outside.

CANTER LENGTHENING

*(E.g. **MBF** progressively show some lengthened strides [in working canter right]. At **F** working canter.)*

The competitor prepares the horse for the lengthened canter by riding him well into the corner before **M**. He then checks the canter is straight by positioning the horse into a *very slight* canter shoulder-fore for a few strides.

The rider asks the horse to lengthen the canter strides with forward-asking seat/leg aids after **M** into an 'uphill' canter lengthening (*see below*). The contact is kept but, as the canter lengthens, the rider's hands let the horse stretch his head and neck a little in front of the vertical by allowing the elbows to move a little forwards towards the horse's mouth and by keeping him soft on the contact.

The rider brings the horse to the working canter before F through repeated half-halts in the rhythm of the canter until the tempo of the working canter is resumed (normally 2–3 strides).

To check straightness and engagement after this exercise, the rider again positions the horse in a slight canter shoulder-fore.

> ### DAVID'S TIP
>
> The emphasis is on 'progressively' in that the judge prefers to see a handful of well-balanced lengthened steps than a horse out of balance and struggling to lengthen the canter strides the full length of the arena. Shoulder-fore and shoulder-in are ridden in similar ways but shoulder-fore is the easier movement.

The judge expects to see that the canter remains straight, the balance remains intact throughout the movement (particularly that the horse does not fall onto his forehand in the transitions), that the horse moves in good rhythm in the upward and downward transitions between the working and lengthened canter and that correct inside bend is maintained.

REIN-BACK

The rein-back often comprises two movements and is marked accordingly. *(E.g. 1. At **C** halt. Immobility for four seconds. 2. At **C** rein-back 3–4 steps [or one horse's length]. **CHS** medium walk.)*

The competitor has approached the halt and rein-back from the left working trot from **M**. The horse is kept in balance through a well-ridden corner and half-halted into a square halt at **C**. The rider sits quietly and maintains the immobility, counting the four seconds. The horse is kept on the aids and attentive. Then the rider quietly lightens his seat, slides his lower legs back behind the girth and applies them softly on the horse's sides, asking him to go 'forwards' into the rein-back but, just as the horse is about to respond to the forward leg aids, the rider squeezes both

his hindquarters, over his back to the bit so that he stands square on all four legs, that he remains attentive during the halt, preserves his immobility for the full four seconds and moves forwards willingly into the next movement. In the rein-back the judge expects to see that the horse does not resist the aids (by resisting the bit, coming above the bit, not stepping backwards willingly nor moving forwards too quickly), so that the rein-back is straight and the diagonal rein-back steps are of equal length, and that the transition to medium walk is active and on the aids.

Here the horse is above the bit and the rein-back is crooked.

reins with equal pressure which asks the horse to step back into the rein-back. The rider repeats these aids so that the rein-back steps flow smoothly one after the other for 3–4 steps. The rider then slides both lower legs forwards onto the girth and applies the aids for the horse to move forwards into medium walk.

The judge expects to see that, in the halt, the horse moves into it actively, remaining straight and allowing the energy to come from

---

DAVID'S TIP

It is important for the rider to always think of the rein-back as a forward-moving exercise. Also, that the synchronization of the aids, smoothly applied, assist the horse in performing the movement well. The steps in rein-back should appear as diagonal pairs without the feet dragging.

ELEMENTARY

COLLECTED TROT

(E.g. FV collected trot.)

The competitor achieves collection by developing the horse's working trot through transitions (e.g. walk to trot, halt to trot and trot to halt) half-halts and exercises such as the shoulder-in. The result is that the horse can easily maintain self-carriage in the collected trot by being ridden forwards with contained energy. This can be achieved by the rider applying the half-halt aids whilst in working trot until the rider feels the horse lift more above the ground (elevation) and, because of the extra lift, the strides cover less ground than those in working trot. The horse must give the feel that he is taking the rider forwards.

The horse in the top photo shows good balance in collected trot.

The judge expects to see that the horse is always active and taking himself and the rider forwards.

Common faults

In the middle photo the neck is 'short' and 'tight' indicating that the rider is pulling on the reins; the horse is neither in self-carriage nor working forwards from his hindquarters. The bottom photo shows trailing hocks; the horse lacks engagement and there is not enough hind leg activity or use of his back.

DAVID'S TIP

The rider must never pull on the reins, block the movement through the horse's back by unbalanced riding or shorten the trot steps in the mistaken belief that this is collection. This is incorrect riding and does not allow the energy through to a more elevated way of going. Collection does not mean going more slowly.

MEDIUM TROT

(E.g. KXM change rein at medium trot. At M collected trot.)

The competitor refreshes the collection in the corner before K asking for the medium trot to go exactly from marker to marker, i.e. from K straight through X to M.

This horse demonstrates a good medium trot. Ideally, his nose should be a little more to the vertical.

Re-engaging the collected trot

The competitor applies the half-halt for collection so that it takes effect exactly at M and then lightens the contact so that the horse develops self-carriage.

Here the horse shows collection.

The judge expects to see that the medium trot is accurate, ridden from marker to marker, that the steps are elevated, of equal length and cover the ground more than the lengthened trot steps, that the horse remains in balance but lengthens his frame to match the strides and that an active trot is maintained in the collection.

COLLECTED CANTER

The competitor develops collection in canter in a similar way to the collected trot using half-halts and both progressive and direct transitions, i.e. trot – canter – trot or walk – canter – walk. It is important that the energy of the canter is maintained through the rider's supple seat and not through heavy rein aids. At all times, the rider wants to feel the horse's back rounding under his seat.

The judge expects to see elevated collected canter in self-carriage.

Common faults

A croup high canter (*see top photo on page 17*): the horse is short in the neck (i.e. restricted in the head and neck) which unbalances the horse onto his shoulders, and lacks activity in the canter thus losing the clear three-beat rhythm.

leading leg to the outside of the arena. *(E.g. EK collected canter left, KD half-circle left 10 m diameter returning to the track at E. ES counter canter. At S collected trot.)*

The competitor rides the horse in left collected canter and is approaching **K**. From **K** to **D** a 10 m half-circle brings the rider straight back to the track at **E**. The horse remains in canter left and is, in effect, in left counter canter from **E** to **S**. The rider stays in the same position for the counter-canter left and is careful not to shift the weight to the right. As in all counter-canter work, the flexion is kept to the same side as true canter and the rhythm of the counter canter remains consistent to the canter gait. At **S** a transition to collected trot is ridden, the flexion is straightened and the new flexion to the right introduced.

COUNTER CANTER

Counter canter is used in competitions to test the obedience and suppleness of the horse. In Novice tests the counter-canter exercises are simple (*see* page 12) but at Elementary level, it progresses into a movement in its own right. In counter canter the horse canters with the

Below are examples of the horse: keeping the correct flexion to the outside (a); showing too much flexion and falling away from the inside leg (b); cutting off the corner in an attempt to evade the counter-canter exercise (c).

Counter canter around the track
(E.g. EHCR counter canter.)

The competitor arrives at the track at E in left canter and keeps the bend over the leading leg and the rhythm of the canter intact. The exercise is finished at R. Care should be taken, as in all counter-canter exercises, not to upset the horse's balance and if this occurs do not ride deep into the corner.

Counter canter loops
(E.g. FM one loop 5 m in from the track.)

The competitor rides the loop in the same way as the trot loop (explained on page 6) but when passing B, the bend is kept over the left leading leg and the counter canter is from B to M. The rider must be careful between B and M not to shift the weight on to the incorrect seatbone which would unbalance the horse. The rider's inside leg asks the horse to return to the track. This tests his acceptance of the inside leg and outside rein.

The judge expects to see 1. that the rhythm of the counter canter stays the same as the true canter; 2. that the bend is kept to the leading leg; 3. that the canter remains on two tracks; 4. that the movement is accurate, e.g. in counter canter around the track the rider keeps the horse on the track; 5. that the horse does not fall away from the rider's inside leg, which would cause him to lose balance and the movement to go out through the outside shoulder; 6. that there is good acceptance of the outside rein.

SIMPLE CHANGE OF CANTER LEAD

(E.g. At B turn right. At X simple change of leg. At E track left.)

Step 1 – the canter

The competitor collects the canter a little from the working canter by half-halting and applies inside leg to outside rein before the turn at B. The canter is kept springy with the seat and leg aids.

This horse is showing collected canter ready for the turn at the B marker.

Step 2 – the walk transition

The competitor uses half-halts to bring the horse into a walk transition. The bend is straightened and the new bend to the left asked for as the horse makes a few steps in medium walk.

Step 3 – walk to new canter lead

The competitor asks for the new left canter lead directly from the walk. The canter is kept springy and active and a half-halt, inside leg to outside rein, prepares the horse for a good turn at **E**.

The judge expects to see that the balance of the canter remains good during the turns across the arena and during the simple change; that the horse is on the aids in the downwards and upwards transitions, e.g. stays 'round' to the bridle and steps into the walk–canter transition immediately without any jogging steps.

These photos were not taken during specific tests. They show (*top*) a good walk transition from canter and (*below*) a bad transition with the horse above the bit, hollow and jogging.

> ### DAVID'S TIP
>
> The simple change is through walk – the upward transition must be directly from walk to canter. However, at Elementary level the *downward transition* may be progressive i.e. canter, trot, walk.

TROT SHOULDER-IN

*(E.g. **KH** shoulder-in right.)*

The competitor must ensure that the trot through the short side of the arena is energetic and balanced. He prepares the horse by riding the corner with correct inside flexion and applies the half halt as he comes out of the corner. This stops the horse from turning in too much and creating too large an angle, which blocks impulsion and fluency of the rhythm. The inside leg is applied at the girth and the outside leg is carried behind the girth, but it is only used if the rider needs to control the hindquarters (i.e. stop them swinging out). The rider brings his inside shoulder back, inside hip forwards and both hands over to the inside which guides the horse's shoulders in from the track so that the outside shoulder is brought in line with the inside hind leg and he comes onto three tracks. The rider's inside leg creates the body bend and encourages the horse forward down the track. The rider's hips and shoulders should be parallel to those of the horse. To straighten the horse after the movement the rider should turn to face down the track and take both hands back in front of him to guide the forehand onto the track.

This horse shows good flexion (*above right*) and bend (*bottom right*) through the body for shoulder-in but the rider has her inside leg slightly too far behind the girth which is pushing the quarters over and making the shoulder-in slightly more than three-track. If the rider brings her inside leg back, the quarters will be pushed over and the exercise is reduced to a leg yield. To keep a good shoulder-in, make sure the inside leg is positioned on, or slightly in front of, the girth.

The judge expects to see that the collected trot remains active and in good rhythm before and during the shoulder-in; that the horse shows increased engagement with his inside hind leg, and the forehand becomes more elevated; that the lateral steps are fluid and of equal length; that the shoulder-in is accurate, i.e. starts and finishes at the requested markers, and is consistently correct with the horse showing the same degree of inside bend, bend through the body and angle of shoulder-in throughout the movement, and that this is the same on both left and right shoulder-in. At Elementary level the shoulder-in is normally asked for along the track and for no more than half the length of a full-sized arena.

This horse is moving on four tracks in a leg yield. There is not enough bend through the body for shoulder-in and the hind legs are crossing.

Here there is too much neck bend and not enough angle which is causing a loss of balance and the outside shoulder is falling out.

YOUNG HORSE TESTS

These tests promote the quality of the dressage training and the talents of the horses rather than emphasizing the accuracy of test riding. Young Horse tests have a specifically designed pattern which encourage the horse to show his best. These development classes are structured around specific movements but the marks are not awarded for the performance of each movement. Instead, the judge studies the quality of the three gaits, the impulsion and submission and awards a collective mark out of ten. For talented young horses this is a terrific bonus because they stand a real chance of being selected as winners on how they move in the three gaits of walk, trot and canter rather than being hindered, and then penalized, by the choreography of the test.

DAVID'S TIP

The horse's 'way of going' is how he moves in the three gaits, how he steps through. Is it a supple, elastic way of going? Does it have balance, energy and star quality? This is what the judge wants to see.

This horse is tense through his back and poll and the collected steps are slightly hovering.

RESULTS ANALYSIS

Using dressage competition constructively adds good dimensions to training the horse and, in addition, brings better results for the competitor. This is especially true for riders who study their competition results. Analysing the test sheet's comments and marks enables you to understand what went right, and why, and what went wrong, and why.

WAY-OF-GOING MISTAKES

Identifying whether the rider is losing marks because of the horse's way of going allows training mistakes to be highlighted. These mistakes will need to be corrected through good quality training. Examples of way-of-going mistakes are: the horse is on the forehand (*see below*), a lack of straightness, an irregular rhythm and the horse is not accepting the contact. These are some of the problems that can occur throughout the test.

TEST-RIDING ERRORS

Marks will be lost when the test has not been ridden as well as it could have been, for example, lack of accuracy, i.e. when the horse strikes off into the wrong canter lead, or the rider asks for the wrong bend. Test-riding errors are easy to correct and the rider can quickly gain better marks in future competitions.

GETTING GOOD RESULTS

Usually, competitors lose marks because of a combination of both types of mistakes. Achieving good results demands honesty. By acknowledging mistakes and working to correct them, the competitor has the opportunity to be more successful in dressage competitions.

DAVID'S TIP

The judge must place the competitors in the correct order of merit. To do this, he awards marks from 0–10 (and in most instances justifies each mark with a comment) for each movement throughout the test, this includes the collective marks. These cover the general impressions of the gaits, impulsion, submission and the effects of the rider. The judge expects to see: rhythm, suppleness, acceptance of the bridle, impulsion, straightness, collection and a good rider position.

The dressage arena

This diagram shows an international-size arena of 20 m x 60 m in which most dressage tests would take place, but many Preliminary and Novice, and some Elementary, tests are performed in 20 m x 40 m arenas

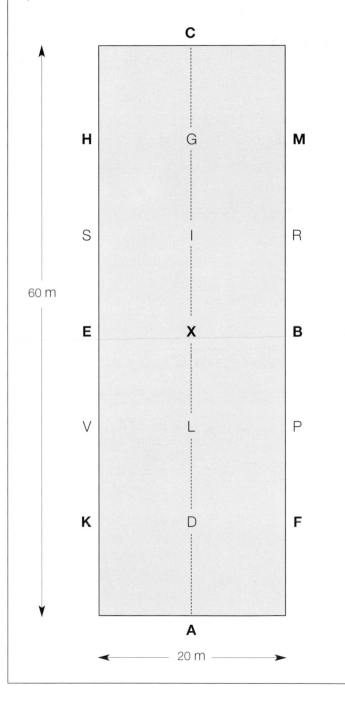

ACKNOWLEDGEMENTS

Special thanks to Douglas Hibbert riding Mrs Leslie Darvas' part Trakehner gelding, Hampton, by Paisley Court. Also to Beverly Brightman with her young horse, the bay mare, Brilliance (Hannoverian by Benz) and her grey Hannoverian gelding, Arlequin. The photographs were taken at Addington Equestrian Centre, many thanks for the use of the Centre's facilities. Thanks also to British Dressage; the test examples are based on their competition test sheets.

British Library Cataloguing-in-Publication Data.
A catalogue record for this book is available from the British Library

ISBN 0.85131.808.8

Published in Great Britain in 2001 by
J. A. Allen an imprint of Robert Hale Ltd.,
Clerkenwell House, 45–47 Clerkenwell Green,
London EC1R 0HT

Reprinted 2004

Design and Typesetting by Paul Saunders
Series editor Jane Lake
Colour processing by Tenon & Polert Colour Processing Ltd., Hong Kong
Printed in Malta by Gutenberg Press Ltd.